NATIONAL SECURITY BENEFITS OF TRADE AGREEMENTS WITH ASIA AND EUROPE

HEARING

BEFORE THE

SUBCOMMITTEE ON TERRORISM, NONPROLIFERATION, AND TRADE

OF THE

COMMITTEE ON FOREIGN AFFAIRS HOUSE OF REPRESENTATIVES

ONE HUNDRED FOURTEENTH CONGRESS

FIRST SESSION

MARCH 17, 2015

Serial No. 114–11

Printed for the use of the Committee on Foreign Affairs

Available via the World Wide Web: http://www.foreignaffairs.house.gov/ or http://www.gpo.gov/fdsys/

U.S. GOVERNMENT PUBLISHING OFFICE

93–818PDF   WASHINGTON : 2015

For sale by the Superintendent of Documents, U.S. Government Publishing Office
Internet: bookstore.gpo.gov   Phone: toll free (866) 512–1800; DC area (202) 512–1800
Fax: (202) 512–2104   Mail: Stop IDCC, Washington, DC 20402–0001

COMMITTEE ON FOREIGN AFFAIRS

EDWARD R. ROYCE, California, *Chairman*

CHRISTOPHER H. SMITH, New Jersey
ILEANA ROS-LEHTINEN, Florida
DANA ROHRABACHER, California
STEVE CHABOT, Ohio
JOE WILSON, South Carolina
MICHAEL T. McCAUL, Texas
TED POE, Texas
MATT SALMON, Arizona
DARRELL E. ISSA, California
TOM MARINO, Pennsylvania
JEFF DUNCAN, South Carolina
MO BROOKS, Alabama
PAUL COOK, California
RANDY K. WEBER SR., Texas
SCOTT PERRY, Pennsylvania
RON DeSANTIS, Florida
MARK MEADOWS, North Carolina
TED S. YOHO, Florida
CURT CLAWSON, Florida
SCOTT DesJARLAIS, Tennessee
REID J. RIBBLE, Wisconsin
DAVID A. TROTT, Michigan
LEE M. ZELDIN, New York
TOM EMMER, Minnesota

ELIOT L. ENGEL, New York
BRAD SHERMAN, California
GREGORY W. MEEKS, New York
ALBIO SIRES, New Jersey
GERALD E. CONNOLLY, Virginia
THEODORE E. DEUTCH, Florida
BRIAN HIGGINS, New York
KAREN BASS, California
WILLIAM KEATING, Massachusetts
DAVID CICILLINE, Rhode Island
ALAN GRAYSON, Florida
AMI BERA, California
ALAN S. LOWENTHAL, California
GRACE MENG, New York
LOIS FRANKEL, Florida
TULSI GABBARD, Hawaii
JOAQUIN CASTRO, Texas
ROBIN L. KELLY, Illinois
BRENDAN F. BOYLE, Pennsylvania

AMY PORTER, *Chief of Staff*   THOMAS SHEEHY, *Staff Director*
JASON STEINBAUM, *Democratic Staff Director*

SUBCOMMITTEE ON TERRORISM, NONPROLIFERATION, AND TRADE

TED POE, Texas, *Chairman*

JOE WILSON, South Carolina
DARRELL E. ISSA, California
PAUL COOK, California
SCOTT PERRY, Pennsylvania
REID J. RIBBLE, Wisconsin
LEE M. ZELDIN, New York

WILLIAM KEATING, Massachusetts
BRAD SHERMAN, California
BRIAN HIGGINS, New York
JOAQUIN CASTRO, Texas
ROBIN L. KELLY, Illinois

CONTENTS

NATIONAL SECURITY BENEFITS OF TRADE AGREEMENTS WITH ASIA AND EUROPE

TUESDAY, MARCH 17, 2015

House of Representatives,
Subcommittee on Terrorism, Nonproliferation, and Trade,
Committee on Foreign Affairs,
Washington, DC.

The committee met, pursuant to notice, at 2 o'clock p.m., in room 2172 Rayburn House Office Building, Hon. Ted Poe (chairman of the subcommittee) presiding.

Mr. POE. The subcommittee will come to order. Without objection, all members may have 5 days to submit statements, questions, and extraneous materials for the record subject to the limitation in the rules. I will now introduce myself for 5 minutes for an opening statement, and then the ranking member will give his opening statement.

I am from the State of Texas. I live in the Houston area and trade is the life blood of my district. Over half of Houston, Texas' economy depends upon the Port of Houston. Many people don't know that, even in Texas. And study after study has shown that the more we trade, the more jobs there are in the United States for Americans. The Port of Houston is an export port. We export everything from fuel to little widgets that make valves in foreign countries. Trade is more than just a market access and jobs. Trade is a key part of foreign policy. It is also part of, I believe, national security.

One of the biggest reasons why we won the Cold War is because our economic model was so much better than that of the Communist system. People around the world compared our economy to the Soviet Union's and could see the difference and where the U.S. was the beacon of freedom and free enterprise, the USSR was all about government control. And when the U.S. opened up trade around the world, USSR closed itself off.

Countries now in Asia are eager to reduce their economic dependence upon China. They don't like Beijing's economic model. They would much rather have a region based upon free market principles. TPP is our opportunity to move into the region in a free market direction and compete with China. It is much better if the United States takes the lead in writing the economic rules for the 21st century in Asia than if China did. China steals intellectual property. It has state-owned enterprises that get unfair subsidies from the central government and it would not seem to me to be wise for the Chinese model to expand in Asia.

(1)

The trade agreement written by China is going to be a lot worse for American interest than if we write it. If we don't get TPP accomplished, it is just not an economic price that we pay. We would essentially be telling Asia that the United States is not interested in Asia. Asian countries will basically have no choice but to look to China as a trading partner.

But there are also other strategic advantages for TPP. The more economically connected we become in Asia, the closer cooperation opens up in other areas like counterterrorism. For example, Malaysia has had a problem with ISIS supporters. With strong trade, we give governments with such types of ISIS problems an incentive to work together on those kinds of tough problems and solve them together. TPP is a chance for the United States to show Asia that we care. Asia does not have to submit to China's ways, and know that we can work together. But most importantly, TPP is a credit for the United States.

A free trade deal the United States is negotiating with the European Union, known as TTIP, offers similar strategic advantages. Even more aggressive than China, Russia took over the sovereign territory of Ukraine. I have met with the Ambassadors of other countries in the Baltics. The Bulgarians, and Romanians feel like they could be next for Russian aggression. One of the reasons why it has been so hard to cooperate with the EU on these issues is that Russia uses Europe's dependence on Russia for energy to blackmail Europe. Countries like Latvia, Finland, and Sweden get 100 percent of their natural gas from Russia. Twelve countries in the EU get over half their natural gas from Russia, so Russia threatens Europe to get to them to do what Moscow wants.

Right now in the United States there is more natural gas than we can use, but the United States Government will not allow American companies to export natural gas. The only exceptions are for companies exporting to a country with whom we have a free trade agreement or companies that get special approval from the Department of Energy.

The Department of Energy approval process has been slow, so slow that drillers have stopped drilling because they know they can't sell it. The long-term solution to this problem is to get American companies sell natural gas around the world, but, in the meantime, if we get TTIP done that also means we can export LNG eventually to every country in the European Union and Russia would no longer have a stranglehold over Europe. No longer would Europe be reluctant to get tougher with Russia and their aggression. This is just one strategic advantage of TTIP. I think there are others.

Finally, TTIP and TPP could help push the world toward greater liberalization. Formal global trade negotiations in Doha are on hold, but together TTIP and TPP represent 90 percent of the world's GDP. These pacts help set the global standard. And countries who do not want to be left out would have to agree to the tough standards set by these agreements in order to enjoy the benefits.

Trade agreements have a geopolitical effect far beyond trade itself. I will now yield to the ranking member, Mr. Keating from Massachusetts, for his 5-minute opening statement.

Mr. KEATING. Thank you, Chairman Poe, for holding today's hearing. And while I believe that there is a link between trade and national security, I do not think that this correlation should outweigh other serious concerns. For example, when the existential need to counterbalance China exists, the fact remains that several of the countries participating in the Trans-Pacific Partnership, or TPP, negotiations remain stark violators of core international standards. In fact, despite claims that this agreement will better protect workers, at least four of the major countries included in TPP are already out of compliance with the international labor organizations' core labor standards.

In Mexico, Malaysia, Vietnam, and Brunei, workers face on-going and systematic abuse with each of them out of compliance. I am additionally skeptical of the TPP agreement that goes without meaningfully addressing currency manipulation, protecting domestic manufacturers, banning commercial whaling, and ensuring transparency.

Further, I am still unsure of what benefits this agreement would bring to the U.S. Just last week, a record breaking $3-billion deficit with Korea was announced by the Census Bureau. These deficits equate to job losses and as we approach the 3-year anniversary of the signing of the U.S.-Korea free trade agreement, the numbers do not bode well for the future of TPP. Quite frankly, there is still a lot left to be desired with TPP and I am not sure the potential national security benefits are worth the sacrifice to American families.

Yet, one trade agreement, if negotiated with global standards in line, may provide new means to uphold the norms that underpin the international trading system. The Transatlantic Trade and Investment Partnership, or TTIP, has remarkable potential to promote economic growth and create jobs throughout the United States and European Union. Since this agreement is between two economies that share a strong commitment to the rule of law, transparency, and free markets, it can help elevate health, safety, labor, and environmental standards worldwide. Beyond trade and investment, TTIP, also has significant strategic implications. The importance of the Transatlantic Alliance has been underscored by Russia's invasion of Ukraine, its increasing hostility toward neighboring states, and the continued decline of fundamental rights and a rule of law under the Putin regime.

The strengthening ties between the United States and the EU that would result from TTIP would only complement the united front that the U.S. and the EU have maintained throughout the Ukraine crisis. TTIP would highlight the virtues of the Western model and send a powerful signal to Putin and other authoritarian regimes that the United States and Europe remain as united as they ever were.

Further, our commitment to higher standards and basic democratic principles is the basis for our prosperity, and that prosperity is our best defense against governments that seek to destabilize international order.

To conclude, Mr. Chairman, I think that the trade discussions cannot be black and white. They should be as varied as the countries and standards and the opportunities represented in agreements themselves. And I look forward to today's discussion and with that, I yield back.

Mr. POE. I thank the gentleman. The chair will now recognize the gentleman—I started to say UCLA, but I better say just California, Mr. Issa, for his opening statement. One minute per member.

Mr. ISSA. Thank you, Mr. Chairman, and Ambassador, I did fail to mention you are LA born, so perhaps UCLA is legitimate. I am not going to get in the middle of that.

Chairman, I thank you for this important hearing. And in brief, I agree more with Mr. Keating's comments than I normally would. The fact is you cannot look at trade agreements in the light only of the trade or all of them being equal. We do have to look at labor laws, rule of law, and of course, the global war on terror slash whatever other names you want to put on it. We have to look at defense cooperation. We have to basically even the playing field with all of our trade agreements. Most of our trade agreements, including the one that I testified as a civilian which was NAFTA during the Bush and early Clinton years, were, in fact, about two of our closest neighbors on which we had very few of these other issues to decide. But I look forward to hearing from our witnesses. I join with the chairman and the ranking member in saying that global free trade is essential. We need to compete with China, but we also need to compete with people that we can rely on in a number of areas. I thank the chairman for his indulgence and yield back.

Mr. POE. The chair will yield a minute to the other gentleman from California, Mr. Sherman.

Mr. SHERMAN. Trade is critically important. That is why we have to get it right which is hard to do when those in power in our country benefit so much whenever we get it wrong. We are told that we should be proud of the trade rules because we wrote them. Yes, we wrote these trade rules and now we should be as proud of them as the citizens of Madrid are of the Spanish flu. We made the trade rules so that we will be making nothing else in the United States. This deal is so bad economically, they are trying to sell it on national security grounds. But what does it do? It entrenches China two ways. First, we have given up on currency manipulation. Why? Just because we don't mention currency manipulation does not mean the Chinese are cheating less. I have only been married a few years, but I am told that I shouldn't——

Mr. POE. Don't go there. Just don't go there.

Mr. SHERMAN. I shouldn't use that line with my wife. ''Honey, I am cheating less'' probably wouldn't do me any good. Second, because of the rules of origin, we are going to see products 50, 60, and really 80 and 90 percent made in China with free access to the United States' market, and us getting no access there. It is time for us to stand up for American security that includes our economic security. It is time for us not to juxtapose these bad deals against the status quo, but these bad deals and the status quo against fair trade, against real results-oriented trade agreements designed to bring our trade deficit to zero within 10 years. I yield back.

Mr. POE. The chair recognizes Mr. Perry for a minute.

Mr. PERRY. I thank the chairman for holding this important hearing. I don't know if the record should reflect that the gentleman from California just admitted that he is cheating, but it seems like in a way——

Mr. SHERMAN. Less. Less.

Mr. PERRY. Oh, less. So important, right, exactly.

Mr. SHERMAN. If China gets our way with it, well, maybe not.

Mr. PERRY. Generally, when we talk about trade agreements in Congress, the media and a lot of people focus on limited, purely the economic implications. And while the economics of trade are obviously important, there is a subtle, but unquestionable geostrategic value associated with these global economic partnerships. For example, along with the other actions with our partners, the strategic value of giving our European allies an alternative to Russian gas through American LNG and the now realized cost of not doing so cannot be understated. With that, I am pleased to be here to receive your input on this topic of great importance and I yield back.

Mr. POE. The gentleman yields back. Does anyone else wish to be recognized for an opening statement? Ms. Kelly? All right, I will now introduce the witnesses that we have before us.

Ambassador Carla Hills is the co-chair of the Council on Foreign Relations and chairperson and CEO of Hills & Company International Consultants. Ambassador Hills has previously served as United States Trade Representative and as Secretary of the Department of Housing and Urban Development.

Dr. Michael Green is senior vice president for Asia and Japan chair of the Center for Strategic and International Studies. Dr. Green is also associate professor at the Edmund A. Walsh School of Foreign Service at Georgetown University.

And Dr. Dan Hamilton is the Austrian Marshall Plan Foundation professor and director of the Center for Transatlantic Relations at the Paul H. Nitze School of Advanced International Studies at Johns Hopkins University. Dr. Hamilton is an award-winning author on the Transatlantic Economy and has previously held a variety of senior U.S. Government positions.

Ambassador Hills, we will start with you. You have 5 minutes.

STATEMENT OF THE HONORABLE CARLA A. HILLS, CO-CHAIRMAN, COUNCIL ON FOREIGN RELATIONS (FORMER U.S. TRADE REPRESENTATIVE)

Ambassador HILLS. Mr. Chairman, Mr. Ranking Member, and members of the committee, I thank you for inviting me to give you my point of view on the national security implications of free trade agreements and the importance that Trade Promotion Authority has on our nation's ability to conclude effective agreements.

Our nations' experience shows that free trade agreements have a positive effect on our national security interests. Free trade agreements stimulates economic growth. As economist Gary Hufbauer at the Peterson Institute for International Economics calculates that the opening of our markets since World War II has increased our nation's GDP by roughly $1 trillion. That increase in economic strength has contributed substantially to our nation's ability to maintain the strongest defense capability in the world.

The opening of markets has also strengthened the economies of our major allies and brought us closer together on a number of issues.

Developing countries have benefitted as well. According to studies by Dr. William Cline at the Center for Global Development, the removal of trade barriers on goods produced by developing countries has a direct correlation to their success in reducing poverty. And according to his calculations, on average, when a developing country increases its ratio of trade to its total output by just 1 percent, it achieves a 1-percent reduction in its level of poverty. And reducing global poverty through trade agreement not only advances our development goals, it creates for us, as did our Marshall Plan, new economic opportunities.

In addition, the negotiation of trade agreements with poorer countries helps to avoid or reduce potential national security challenges, for failure to enlarge their economic opportunities makes them more susceptible to recruitment by those who would do us harm.

Also impoverished nations often lose the ability to enforce their laws or secure their borders, making it more difficult for our Government to deal with security problems like terrorism. And enlarging their opportunities reduces their potential for instability which advances our national security interests.

Continuing to build on our nation's economic strength through strong trade agreements with countries rich and poor will help ensure that we have the necessary resources going forward to support equipment, technology, and manpower we need to protect our security interests.

And Trade Promotion Authority, TPA, is a critical tool to enable our Government to negotiate good and strong agreements. Our Constitution vests the Congress the power to regulate commerce, to levy duties, and it vests the Executive branch with the responsibility for negotiating with foreign governments including issues dealing with commercial trade.

TPA sets up a collaborative process used since 1934 when President Roosevelt signed the Reciprocal Trade Act, as a predecessor to TPA, and the Congress has passed a similar bill 18 different times since.

Under these procedures, the President gives Congress notice of trade negotiation. Congress may set objectives for the administration and may ask the administration to consult with it during the course of the administration and in return, Congress agrees to approve or reject, but not amend the trade agreement that the administration presents. Our negotiators cannot achieve the best trade deals if our trade partners expect there will be a second negotiation with Congress. Inevitably, they will hold back the key issues that we want the most in anticipation of that negotiation with Congress.

To reach a good trade agreement requires striking a balance on a broad range of issues that have differing degrees of importance to the governments participating and a single amendment can upset that balance and cause the agreement to unravel. What happens beyond our borders for good or bad has an impact here. We need to make every effort to take actions that will generate good outcomes and minimize the bad and the negotiating of a strong trade agreement will have positive effects on our nation both economically and with respect to our national security. To achieve that benefit requires the Congress to pass Trade Promotion Authority. And I thank you.

[The prepared statement of Ambassador Hills follows:]

Statement of the Honorable Carla A. Hills
Chair & CEO of Hills & Company, International Consultants
U.S. Trade Representative 1989-1993

Before the Committee on Foreign Affairs
Subcommittee on the Western Hemisphere
U.S. House of Representatives

Wednesday, March 17, 2015

"National Security Implications of Free Trade Agreements
And
The Opportunities and Challenges of Trade Promotion Authority"

Mr. Chairman and Members of the Terrorism, Nonproliferation and Trade Subcommittee of the House of Representative's Committee on Foreign Affairs, thank you for inviting me to share my perspective on the national security implications of our free trade agreements and the importance that Trade Promotion Authority has on our nation's ability to conclude effective agreements.

Benefits of U.S. Trade Agreements

Our nation's experience shows that our free trade agreements have a very positive effect on our national security interests in a number of ways. By opening global and regional markets, a free trade agreement stimulates economic growth. Economist Dr. Gary Hufbauer at the Peterson Institute for International Economics calculates that the opening of markets beyond our borders since World War II has increased our nation's GDP by roughly one trillion dollars per year. That increase in economic strength has contributed substantially to our nation's ability to maintain the strongest defense capability in the world.

The opening of markets to trade and investment has strengthened the economies of our major allies, including Europe, Canada, Mexico, Japan, South Korea, and more. It has also brought us closer together on a number of policy issues.

But the benefits that flow from opening global markets are not restricted to the United States and other advanced economies with which we trade and invest most heavily. Developing nations benefit as well. According to studies by Dr. William Cline at the Center for Global Development, the removal of trade barriers to the goods produced by developing countries has a direct correlation to their success in reducing their poverty. According to his calculations on average when a developing country increases its ratio of trade to its total output by one percent, it achieves a one percent reduction in its level of poverty.

Reducing global poverty through trade agreements does not just advance our humanitarian and development goals in an efficient manner. By integrating poorer countries into regional and global trade regimes, we engage in what some have termed "enlightened self-interest" much as we did with the Marshall Plan when we helped to rebuild the European markets following World War II. These countries often become our future trading partners.

In addition the negotiation of trade agreements with poorer countries helps us avoid or reduce potential national security challenges. Failure to enlarge the economic opportunities of these countries condemns segments of their population to unrelieved poverty making them more susceptible to recruitment by those who would do us harm.

Also we know that impoverished nations often lose the ability to enforce their laws and secure their borders, slipping into the status of a failed state making it much more difficult for our government to deal effectively with serious security problems - - - terrorism, organized crime, illegal arms sales, money laundering, and more. By working with emerging economies to enlarge their trade opportunities, we not only enhance their opportunities for economic growth, we reduce their potential for instability that adversely impacts our national security interests.

Continuing to build on our nation's economic strength through good strong trade agreements with countries rich and poor will help ensure that we have the necessary resources going forward to support the equipment, technology, and manpower we need to protect our national security.

Role of Trade Promotion Authority

Trade Promotion Authority, "TPA", is a critical tool to enable our government to negotiate strong agreements to open global and regional markets enabling our nation to support adequately our national security objectives. Our founding fathers separated our government's executive, legislative, and judicial responsibilities. Our Constitution vests in Congress the power to "regulate commerce with foreign nations" and to "lay and collect taxes, duties, imposts, and excises", and vests in the Executive the responsibility for negotiating treaties with foreign governments, including those dealing with commercial issues.

TPA sets up a cooperative process that enables the two branches of government to reach strong trade agreements. This collaboration between the executive and legislative branches has existed since 1934 when President Roosevelt signed the Reciprocal Trade Agreements Act, a predecessor of TPA. Since then Congress has passed 18 such bills.

Under these procedures, the President gives Congress notice of a trade negotiation. Congress in the exercise of its constitutional power to regulate commerce may set objectives for the Administration to seek and ask that the Administration consult with it during the course of the negotiation. In return Congress agrees to approve or reject - - - but not amend - - - the trade agreement that the Administration presents. The assurance that Congress will not amend the agreement that the President presents is based on a recognition that our negotiators could not achieve the best trade deals if our trade partners expected that there would be a second negotiation with Congress. Inevitably they would hold back on key issues that we wanted in anticipation of a further negotiation with Congress.

Also, since trade agreements typically cover hundreds of issues, each of the participants looks at how the whole agreement affects his or her national interests. To be successful our trade negotiators must strive to strike a balance on a broad range of issues that have differing degrees of importance to the governments participating. A single amendment can upset that balance and cause the agreement to unravel.

Conclusion

Globalization exposes us to economic and geostrategic issues occurring worldwide. What happens beyond our border, for good and bad, has an impact here. We need to make every effort to take actions that will generate good outcomes and minimize the bad. The negotiation of strong trade agreements will have positive effects for our nation both economically and with respect to our national security. To secure good trade agreements requires that Congress and the President work together. Trade Promotion Authority has shown itself for more than 80 years to be the proven method for the Legislative and Executive branches of our government to do just that and achieve outstanding results. To maximize economic growth both domestically and globally and to obtain the national security benefits that flow from that growth, we need to continue to seek to open markets around the world. That will require Congress to pass Trade Promotion Authority.

Mr. POE. Thank you, Ambassador. Dr. Green.

STATEMENT OF MICHAEL J. GREEN, PH.D., SENIOR VICE PRESIDENT FOR ASIA AND JAPAN CHAIR, CENTER FOR STRATEGIC AND INTERNATIONAL STUDIES

Mr. GREEN. Thank you, Mr. Chairman. I am here to talk about the geostrategic importance of the Trans-Pacific Partnership, TPP, but I want to begin by making the point that we are not talking about a case with TPP where we need to sacrifice our economic interests in order to advance our geopolitical interests. There are geopolitical advantages that are significant, but it is also likely to be a very good economic deal.

These are countries, Japan, Vietnam, and others that have not traditionally been so open. Now they are stuck. Their old model of growth isn't working and they want to reduce their dependence on China. And the leverage is largely with us. We will write the rules and the estimates by the Peterson Institute and others are that liberalization through TPP will add 0.4 percent to our GDP, the U.S. GDP over the next decade. That is a lot of money. So it is likely to be a good economic deal. But let me tell you why it is important geostrategically to our interests in Asia.

First, at CSIS, at my think tank, we did a survey of leading political thought with leaders across Asia. And we asked what they thought about President Obama's promise to rebalance or pivot to the Asia Pacific region. And outside of China, well over 80 percent said they wanted more of the United States and they supported this. But well over half said they had doubts that we could actually execute.

Our ability to pass TPA and TPP, and for the Congress and the administration to get this done goes right to the heart of U.S. credibility in the region as a whole. And extends even to how seriously our allies take our security commitments and our diplomatic commitments because from their perspective this is so self-evidently in our own economic and strategic interests. So it goes right to the heart of American credibility.

Second, a successful TPP deal will anchor our relationship with Japan. A deal with Japan is likely to create twice as much trade in U.S. exports than a deal without Japan. So it is good for us economically.

For Prime Minister Abe, this is a critical way to jump start what is politically hard for him at home and that is restructuring the Japanese economy to grow. And we want the Japanese economy to grow and to absorb our imports, but also because Japan is now the second largest funder of the IMF, World Bank, most of the international institutions, the United Nations, and the most important host of U.S. bases. We have a stake in Japan growing and leading because we share common values and because Japan with some exceptions, such as their difficult relationship with Korea and China, is quite respected and popular in Asia and the anchor for our presence in the region.

Third, a successful passage of TPA and TPP will decide who over the coming decade writes the rules in Asia. We did another survey at CSIS in 2009 and the majority of Asians thought that the most important rulemaking and trade liberalizing framework for Asia would be RCEP, the Regional Comprehensive Economic Partnership, which includes 16 countries and not us. And it is a China-centered trade arrangement. That was in 2009. Last year when we asked the question what trade architecture or arrangement is most likely to set the norms and the rules, the answer by a large margin was TPP. We have real momentum, particularly since Japan joined. To not pass TPA and TPP would be to slowly pass the baton back to others to decide what the rules will be, what the center of economic growth or the center of economic norms will be. And obviously, we want that to be us.

And finally, an interesting thing is happening in China in response to TPP. A few years ago, the Chinese Government argued that this was an instrument of the United States to contain China and the Chinese lobbied very aggressively in countries like Japan and New Zealand and Vietnam to try to block TPP. When Japan entered the negotiations, the Chinese position shifted. And so for the last 2 years, reformers in China who want changes so that China can have a more effective economy, are arguing that they can use TPP the way China used the World Trade Organization, WTO negotiations, in the 1990s to force change within China. So China is not in the TPP negotiations. Notionally, it could be some day down the road, but immediately passage of TPA and TPP will give us far more leverage, far more purchase as we negotiate difficult issues with China because China will understand this is where the region is going and who is making the rules. Thank you.

[The prepared statement of Mr. Green follows:]

CSIS | CENTER FOR STRATEGIC &
INTERNATIONAL STUDIES

Statement before the House Foreign Affairs Committee

Subcommittee on Terrorism, Nonproliferation and Trade

"TPP AND AMERICAN GRAND STRATEGY IN THE ASIA PACIFIC REGION"

A Statement by:

Dr. Michael Green

Senior Vice President for Asia and Japan Chair,

Center for Strategic and International Studies (CSIS)

Associate Professor, Edmund A. Walsh

School of Foreign Service, Georgetown University

March 17, 2014

2172 Rayburn House Office Building

WWW.CSIS.ORG   1616 RHODE ISLAND AVENUE NW | TEL. (202) 887.0200
WASHINGTON, DC 20036 | FAX (202) 775.3199

Green: TPP Testimony to HFAC   March 17, 2012

Chairman Poe, Majority Leader Keating, Members of the Committee, it is my pleasure to testify today on the national security benefits of the Trans-Pacific Partnership, or TPP, now under negotiation with our key allies and partners in the Asia Pacific region.

From the very beginning of our Republic, trade across the Pacific has been closely linked to our nation's security. In 1784 Robert Morris, dead-broke from financing the continental army of George Washington, outfitted a ship in New York in search of markets not yet closed to us by the British. His first ship, the *Empress of China*, sailed to Canton (today Guangzhou) laden with ginseng from what is today Pennsylvania and West Virginia and returned home with over 400% profits. Soon ships from Boston, Salem, New York and Baltimore were trading sea otter pelts from the Pacific Northwest and sandalwood from Hawaii and staking our claim as a Pacific nation before we had even expanded west beyond the Alleghenies.

In the late 19th Century our greatest naval strategist, Alfred Thayer Mahan, noted that a strong navy alone was not enough to secure the American position in the Pacific. In those days the Republican Party and his friend Theodore Roosevelt were proponents of a high tariff, but Mahan chastised them, arguing that the tariff was like the civil war ironclad ship USS Monitor –suitable for river defense and nothing more. Free trade was the instrument of a great maritime nation, he maintained, like the ocean-going battle cruisers that would soon win the Battle of Manila Bay.

In the 1930s the United States forgot the indispensable role of trade in securing the Pacific and passed the Smoot-Hawley tariffs, cutting Japan's trade with the United States in half and driving Tokyo towards a violent autarkic trading system of its own under the Greater East Asian Co-prosperity Sphere. Even as the U.S. Marines were landing at Iwo Jima to defeat the Empire of Japan and re-open the Pacific, Americans were planning the Bretton Woods system to ensure that post-war order and stability would be underpinned by an open rules-based economic system. That system has never been static –to succeed it must continually be strengthened with new member states drawn in, new markets opened, and the rules updated to reflect new economic realities.

The Trans Pacific Partnership (TPP) represents the most important effort to modernize trade across the Pacific in a generation. The negotiations with Australia, Brunei, Canada, Chile, Japan, Malaysia, Mexico, New Zealand, Peru, Singapore, and Vietnam are almost complete and offer significant economic and trade gains to the United States. The Peterson Institute's 2012 model demonstrates annual economic gains of $77.5 billion in 2025 for the United States in 2007 dollars with an increase of exports by $124 billion. A successful TPP agreement will build on global trading agreements at Doha by expanding into uncovered areas such as services, investment, competition, regulatory coherence. TPP will strengthen investor protection, discipline large state owned enterprises, enhance intellectual property rights protection and integrate the existing "spaghetti bowl" of trading agreements –all making it easier and fairer for large, medium and small U.S. firms to export to the world's most dynamic region.

But as Robert Morris, Alfred Thayer Mahan, or Franklin Delano Roosevelt would add – TPP will also reinforce American strategic interests in the Asia Pacific region at a time of major uncertainty. America turned protectionist in the 1930s just as Japan was emerging as a revisionist power seeking to push the United States out of the Pacific. Today we face a similar, if somewhat more benign circumstance. The United States is more powerful today than we were in the 1930s and Asia is made up of nation states rather than loosely held and vulnerable European colonies as it was before the war. Moreover, most of the states are democratic or transitioning towards democracy.

Nevertheless, China's rhetoric and behavior in the region bear some menacing overtones from previous eras and have rattled neighboring states from India to Japan. Last April in Shanghai, President Xi Jinping called for a "new security order in Asia" without "blocs" –a direct reference to the network of U.S. alliances that have kept the peace since the war. The Peoples Liberation Army budget has increased at double digit growth rates over the past two decades, arming China with new capabilities to challenge the United States in outer-space, cyber-space and the offshore island chain stretching from Japan through the Philippines to the Straits of Malacca. As CSIS demonstrated with previously unavailable footage on our Asia Maritime Transparency Initiative (AMTI) website, China has converted six small rocky crops in the South China Sea into military facilities designed to increase military dominance over smaller countries like the Philippines and Vietnam with which Beijing is contesting control of maritime domain.

At the same time, it is important to emphasize that Beijing still considers the United States to be its most important strategic counterpart and trading partner in the world and Xi has proposed a "New Model of Great Power Relations" with Washington aimed at sharing rather than contesting power in the Pacific. If we were a declining or even static power, such power-sharing might be tempting. In fact, however, we are a nation with unique competitiveness, abundant energy, and allies and partners in the Asia Pacific eager to see us lead. We are therefore positioned to shape a new cooperative relationship with China based not on relaxing the rules and splitting our differences, but instead on a broadening and deepening of the rules that would dissuade China from revisionism and encourage peaceful cooperation and integration down the road.

Successful completion of TPP is central to that mission in three ways.

First, TPP will solidify our key alliances and partnerships. Japan is the linchpin of American presence in the Asia Pacific region, hosting our major air and naval assets and standing as a partner on rule-making and support for democracy and development across the region. When Prime Minster Shinzo Abe decided to join the TPP negotiations in 2013, it energized American exporters and blunted China's efforts to convince smaller countries not to join. Japan has the third largest economy in the world, yet only about 17% of Japanese trade is covered by economic partnerships or free trade agreements. The Abe government has already made significant moves to reform the agricultural sector and the differences in our position with Japan in the negotiations are now small in dollar terms, though politically sensitive. On the rule-making side, we and Japan are essentially on the same page. Japan stands to gain $119 billion annually from TPP according to the

Peterson Institute study. More importantly, TPP would open Japan's market to American and regional imports and investment, adding real momentum to Prime Minister Abe's "third arrow" of structural reform and further aligning Washington and Tokyo for liberalization elsewhere –increasing the incentives for countries like Vietnam and Malaysia to complete negotiations, for Korea to "dock" the KORUS Free Trade Agreement with TPP, and for China to change the arc of its economic policy towards integration with 21st Century rules for trade.

Second, successful TPP negotiations will set the standard for competing trade negotiations in the Asia-Pacific region that do not include the United States. Principal among these is the Regional Comprehensive Economic Partnership (RCEP), which covers the ten ASEAN member countries and six of their major trading partners — China, Japan, India, South Korea, Australia and New Zealand. RCEP has its roots in Malaysian Prime Minister Mohammed Mahathir's concept of an "East Asian Economic Community" which he hoped in the late 1980s would counter the establishment of the Asia Pacific Economic Cooperation (APEC) summits and the North American Free Trade Agreement (NAFTA). With the presence of U.S. allies like Japan and Australia in the talks, RCEP is unlikely to become an anti-U.S. bloc, but the group is dominated by China and other countries that will drive for lower levels of liberalization and a less binding set of rules for state-owned enterprises, labor and the environment. In surveys of Asian elites taken last spring, CSIS found that a majority of experts thought TPP had greater momentum than RCEP. That increases the likelihood that TPP will set higher standards for liberalization and empower countries like Japan, Australia or Singapore that want those Asian-only negotiations to strive for NAFTA-plus outcomes. TPP and RCEP do not necessarily have to be in a zero-sum race against each other –competitive trade liberalization means that those countries counting on lower standards of trade liberalization will be pressed by TPP completion to open more themselves. The net-effect will be rule-making led by Washington in partnership with Tokyo, Canberra and other like-minded states and therefore a regional architecture of institutions that reduces the temptation for rising powers to try to change the rules.

Third, successful TPP negotiations will align the entire region better as China chooses its own economic future. Initially, Beijing was hostile to TPP, charging that the negotiation was aimed at "containing" China by creating a collective security framework like NATO in Asia. Chinese diplomats and proxies actively lobbied against TPP in countries like Japan, Australia and Malaysia. Once Japan joined the negotiations, however, TPP became a force too large for China to blunt. Japan's participation also coincided with a somewhat more ambitious economic reform plan under Xi and Chinese Premier Li Keqiang. Chinese officials began arguing that perhaps TPP would be useful for China's economic reform as a source of external pressure the way WTO succession was in the 1990s as then-Premier Zhu Rongji restructured state-owned enterprises. In the Sunnylands U.S.-China summit last June the Chinese side requested a briefing on TPP. Then as host of APEC last November, Xi Jinping called for moving towards FTAAP –a free trade area of the Asia Pacific tabled in the 2007 Sydney APEC summit. FTAAP would include all the APEC members, among them China. The other TPP members are certainly not ready to include China in the talks yet, but Beijing's recent moves signal that TPP plays a critical role in shaping China's own internal debate about reform and integration with world trading system. Coupled with TTIP, TPP has real potential to not only pull China into modern rule-making, but re-energize global talks at Doha as a whole.

To conclude, one might briefly consider the national security impact should TPP talks completely stall this year. The U.S. economy is strong enough to weather any break-down in trade talks for now, but President Obama's goal of increasing exports would suffer over the longer-term as alternate trade agreements drew to a close without our rules or our membership. Meanwhile, our Asian allies and partners would begin questioning the commitment of the administration and Congress to the Asia Pacific region, including our will power to resist Chinese coercion, North Korean provocations, and backsliding on democratization in Burma/Myanmar. TPP does not offer a specific solution to any of these challenges, but it does indicate how ready we are to continue leading in the region. Japan's stock market would probably react negatively to any break-down of TPP talks and investors would question Prime Minister Abe's commitment to reform and restructuring. A hit to Japanese growth and credibility would be a hit to U.S. strategic interests. China meanwhile, would return to debating its own economic future without the prospect of an over-arching set of global and trans-Pacific rules and institutions that would determine Beijing's own competitiveness and ability to grow. American leadership, trade -- and ultimately security—would suffer.

It would be an exaggeration to say that failure of TPP would amount to another Smoot-Hawley tariff, but a generation from now such a failure could be one of the lost opportunities historians point *back* to should this region fall victim to the great power rivalries of the 19th Century instead of achieving the enormous potential for prosperity of the 21st Century.

Thank you.

––––––––––

Mr. POE. Thank you, Dr. Green. Dr. Hamilton, your opening statement.

STATEMENT OF DANIEL S. HAMILTON, PH.D., DIRECTOR, CENTER FOR TRANSATLANTIC RELATIONS, THE PAUL H. NITZE SCHOOL OF ADVANCED INTERNATIONAL STUDIES, JOHNS HOPKINS UNIVERSITY

Mr. HAMILTON. Thank you, Mr. Chairman. I was asked to speak on the geopolitical implications of the Transatlantic Trade and Investment Partnership, the TTIP, so I will do that. I welcome it because the discussion so far has been very focused on the economic elements of this negotiation and there are considerable other geopolitical elements as both you and Mr. Keating mentioned.

I think it is best to understand the TTIP, not just as another trade agreement, but as a way for the United States and Europe to reposition themselves for the world we are facing, a world of more diffuse economic power, intensified global competition, and how do the core nations of the West act and do they act together in that way?

It seems to me there are three broad areas of which there is a geopolitical national security element to the TTIP beyond the economics. One is about the transatlantic community itself. The second is how we engage rising powers and whether we do it together. And the third is how this will relate to the international rules-based systems, strengthen it or weaken it.

On the first issue, the TTIP is potentially a powerful way to reaffirm the bond across the Atlantic based on our economic base, the geoeconomic base that we both have, $5.5 trillion economy, 15 million workers owe their jobs to the healthy commerce across the Atlantic. No other commercial artery is integrated as that across the Atlantic. We release every year an annual survey of all the jobs, trade, and investment. We are going to do that tomorrow. But I can tell you, Mr. Chairman, in Texas, the latest data show 300,000 jobs directly supported by European investment in Texas and if you take the trade, all the indirect effects, we would estimate over 1 million Texas jobs directly dependent upon healthy commerce with Europe. And you mentioned Houston's export center. Texas exports multiple times more to Europe than it does to China.

The same for Massachusetts, Mr. Keating, about 150,000 jobs are directly due to just European investment in Massachusetts. About 500,000 overall if you put direct and investment together. And I could go on.

There is more for Mr. Sherman, you know, there's more employment in Los Angeles County by European companies than Asian companies. California exports twice as much to Europe as it does to China, a West Coast state.

And for Ms. Kelly in Illinois, 185,000 jobs are directly supported by European investment in Illinois and over 500,000 Illinois jobs are dependent upon healthy commerce with Europe.

So it is our geoeconomic base, if you will. It is also traditionally, of course, our geopolitical partner on so many issues. And yet, there are questions of trust and commitment across the Atlantic these days. NATO is perceived in some quarters to be wobbly. TTIP would be the other side of the coin of our commitment to Europe through our military alliance. And I think particularly given the issues facing European security these days, it is a vital reassurance of the U.S. commitment to Europe.

It also would reassure Americans who wonder about the European Union and whether it is inward or outward looking that the EU would be a very strong outward-looking partner because TTIP would essentially make that case.

The second area is how both of us together relate to rising powers. And Dr. Green mentioned a few of those elements. But I think one has to think about this. Those rising powers are each having debates on how they relate to the international system. Do they challenge it? Do they accommodate themselves to it? And the message we have to those countries as they have those debates is actually quite important.

In recent years, we have had different messages or muddled messages, European messages, American messages. We don't have a message. So TTIP is a single, strong message about a robust, revitalized West, not defensive, but also not aggressive. It is about upholding standards, not eroding them. And it has an impact on each of the countries that we could discuss. Dr. Green mentioned China. It is not about isolating China. It is about defining the terms of China's integration, what standards do we talk about? It is about Russia. TTIP is essentially a reassertion of Western values, robust international law, predictability and commercial contracts, human rights, all of that. That is anathema to Vladimir Putin. And he is conducting what the KGB used to call ''active measures'' to subvert the TTIP because he understands what it means. So it has a huge impact on Russia. It is a symbol of unity.

The last piece is how we together will relate to the international rules-based system. We were the stewards of that system. And so the question of the TTIP is can we again establish standards at a high level that protect our workers, our consumers and labor, or do we allow each of our standards to start to erode because we don't have an agreement? Those are the kinds of things that I believe will strengthen the international system rather than subvert it. Thank you.

[The prepared statement of Mr. Hamilton follows:]

JOHNS HOPKINS
SCHOOL *of* ADVANCED
INTERNATIONAL STUDIES

TTIP's Geostrategic Implications

Testimony by
Daniel S. Hamilton
Executive Director, Center for Transatlantic Relations
Johns Hopkins University SAIS

Hearing on
"National Security Benefits of Trade Agreements with Asia and Europe"
Subcommittee on Terrorism, Non-Proliferation and Trade
Committee on Foreign Affairs
U.S. House of Representatives

March 17, 2015

Chairman Poe, Ranking Member Keating, distinguished members of the Committee, the Transatlantic Trade and Investment Partnership (TTIP) currently under negotiation by the United States and the European Union (EU) promises to unleash significant opportunities to generate jobs, trade and investment across the Atlantic. Yet while much discussion has focused on TTIP's potential economic impact, there has been little exploration of its geostrategic and national security implications.

TTIP is first and foremost an economic negotiation, but it is far more than just another trade agreement. TTIP seeks nothing less than to reposition the U.S. and its European allies and partners for a more diffuse world of intensified global competition.

TTIP is important to U.S. national security and foreign policy in three ways.

First, it has the potential to reinforce America's geostrategic base -- the transatlantic alliance.

Second, it can enable the U.S. and its allies to be more effective when engaging third countries and addressing regional and global challenges.

Third, it can help us strengthen the ground rules of the international order. Let us look at each of these elements in turn.

TTIP and the Transatlantic Alliance

TTIP is politically important to the transatlantic relationship itself. The transatlantic economy generates $5.5 trillion in total commercial sales a year and employs up to 15 million workers. It is the largest and wealthiest market in the world, accounting for three-quarters of global financial markets and over half of world trade. It accounts for over 35% of world GDP in terms of purchasing power. No other commercial artery is as integrated. In many ways, the transatlantic economy is a major geostrategic base for the United States.

TTIP is rooted in a core truth: despite the rise of other powers the United States and Europe remain the fulcrum of the world economy, each other's most important and profitable market and source of onshored jobs, each other's most important strategic partner, each other's closest partner in terms of values, and still a potent force in the multilateral system—when the two partners work in concert. The transatlantic relationship remains a foundational element of the global economy and the essential underpinning of a strong rules-based international order. Americans and Europeans literally cannot afford to neglect it. TTIP is evidence that the two partners are committed to open transatlantic markets, strengthen global rules and leverage global growth.

Despite this strength and potential, the U.S.-EU relationship regularly punches below its weight and fails to capitalize on significant opportunities for American and European citizens, companies, workers, consumers and the multilateral system they helped bring to life. In recent years the relationship has being buffeted by daunting economic challenges on each side of the Atlantic.

Without U.S. fiscal solvency, economic growth, job creation and an end to partisan gridlock, Washington is unlikely to be the type of consistent, outward looking partner that Europeans need and want. The United States has the same stake in Europe's success. Europe's protracted sovereign debt crisis and anemic economic recovery threaten to drain U.S. confidence in Europe and its institutions and derail American support for major transatlantic policy initiatives. The single most important effort the partners could make to improve their ability to act together abroad is for each to get its act together at home. To the extent that TTIP can energize growth and restore mutual confidence, it can help get the relationship back on track.

TTIP can be an operational reflection of basic values shared across the Atlantic. TTIP's fundaments are those of democratic societies rooted in respect for human rights and the rule of law. The United States and the European Union are among the few entities that include basic labor, environmental and consumer protections in their trade agreements. They boast the two most sophisticated regulatory systems in the world. An agreement that commits both parties to sustain and uphold such principles and protections, not only vis-a-vis each other but together around the world, would be a strong affirmation of common values and a powerful instrument to ensure that such standards advance globally.

In all these ways, TTIP can be both a symbolic and practical assertion of Western renewal, vigor and commitment, not only to each other but to high rules-based standards and core principles of international order. It can be assertive, yet need not be aggressive. It challenges fashionable notions about a "weakened West."

TTIP can also serve to reassure each side of the Atlantic about each other. In recent years the transatlantic relationship has been challenged less because either partner assigns lesser value to the same norms, but rather that both have assigned lesser value to each other, due in particular to the shift away from Europe as the central theater of world affairs to a more diffuse world, which is exacerbated by the mix of generational and ethnic change within American politics towards cohorts who put less value on relations with Europe. The challenge is less antipathy than apathy, not more conflict but rather less priority.

This relative inattention had had political consequences. In many quarters NATO is perceived to be wobbly. Moreover, a military alliance is insufficient as the sole anchor to what is a much broader and deeper transatlantic community of values and interests. Many Europeans are worried that the U.S. "pivot" to Asia will translate into less U.S. attention and commitment to Europe. Creation of what would essentially be a Euro-American market, together with a commitment to work together to advance core Western norms and standards, would offer reassurance that Europe is in fact America's "partner of choice" and that the pivot to Asia is not a pivot away from Europe.

Europeans are more likely to have greater faith in America's security commitments if they are anchored by strong trade and investment links. TTIP would also reassure Americans that the European Union is committed to look outward rather than inward. It would provide a new sense of purpose and direction for the transatlantic relationship at a time when transatlantic solidarity has been challenged by Russia's forceful annexation of the Crimean region of Ukraine and its direct military intervention to support armed separatists in other parts of the country.

Some proponents have characterized TTIP as an "economic NATO." This is a mistake that easily invites misinterpretation. In the American political context, the term "economic NATO" can be convenient shorthand to convey that TTIP is about a renewed sense of transatlantic solidarity. But for many Europeans the term doesn't translate so readily. The term's military allusion, for instance, conveys the impression that TTIP is directed against a particular threat, which it is not. In addition, NATO is dominated by one large military superpower, whereas TTIP is comprised of two roughly equal economic entities; references to an "economic NATO" offer unnecessary fodder to European critics concerned that the TTIP is a thinly veiled U.S. effort to assert economic dominance and steamroll the European way of life. And for other Europeans who are worried about America's staying power in Europe, the term raises concern that the United States may be diluting its strategic commitment to Europe in favor of a more transactional commercial partnership. For all of these reasons, TTIP is best characterized as offering a second anchor to the transatlantic partnership, in addition to NATO, and not as an "economic NATO." TTIP and NATO are two sides of the same coin; one cannot substitute for the other.

TTIP is also important to each partner's own goals for itself. The United States, for example, is also negotiating a second mega-regional economic agreement, the Trans-Pacific Partnership, with 11 other Asia-Pacific partners. If TTIP and TPP are successful, the United States and its partners will have opened trade and investment across both the Atlantic and the Pacific with countries accounting for two-thirds of global output. Since the United States is the only party to both initiatives, the negotiations give Washington a distinct advantage in leveraging issues in one forum to advance its interests in the other, while potentially reinvigorating U.S. global leadership.

Terms of Engagement: Working with Other Powers

Second, TTIP is important in terms of how the transatlantic partners together might best relate to rising powers, especially the emerging growth markets. Whether those powers choose to challenge the current international order and its rules or promote themselves within it depends significantly on how the United States and Europe engage, not only with them but also with each other. The stronger the bonds among core democratic market economies, the better their chances of being able to include rising partners as responsible stakeholders in the international system. The more united, integrated, interconnected and dynamic the international liberal order – shaped in large part by the United States and Europe – the greater the likelihood that emerging powers will rise within this order and adhere to its rules. The looser or weaker those bonds are, the greater the likelihood that rising powers will challenge this order. So a key foreign policy goal must be to protect and reinforce the institutional foundations of the international rules-based order, beginning with the partnership between the United States and Europe.

There are already signs that TTIP is affecting third countries such as Brazil and Japan. TTIP was "the elephant in the room" at the last EU-Brazil summit; it is causing Brazilian leaders to reframe how they think of their evolving role and position. Japan's decision to join the TPP arguably was due as much to the start of TTIP negotiations as to inner-Asian dynamics. With the EU now also negotiating a bilateral trade agreement with Japan, both the United States and the EU are in direct talks with Tokyo about opening the Japanese market -- a goal that for decades has seemed unattainable.

TTIP has particular meaning for U.S. and EU relations with China and with Russia.

TTIP is lazily portrayed as an effort to confront and isolate China. Yet is less about containing China than about the terms and principles guiding China's integration and participation in the global economy. China's burgeoning trade with both the United States and Europe attests to U.S. and EU interest in engaging China, not isolating it. Yet Beijing has yet to embrace some basic tenets of the international rules-based order, and has sought to translate its economic clout into military influence, for instance saber-rattling on territorial claims in the South China Sea; or into diplomatic and political influence, for instance by holding down the value of its currency to boost its companies, leveraging its near-monopoly on rare earths to advance its strategic objectives, or directing state-owned companies not just to generate profits but to wield power on its behalf. TTIP, TPP and related initiatives are important instruments to help frame Beijing's choices -- by underscoring China's own interests in an open, stable international system as well as the types of norms and standards necessary for such a system to be sustained. China itself has changed its position and signaled a willingness to join plurilateral talks on services. Its motivations remain unclear, but there is no denying that TTIP and related initiatives are injecting new movement and energy into efforts to open markets and strengthen global rules.

TTIP is also important with regard to U.S. and EU relations with Russia and Eurasia. TTIP is a values-based, rules-based initiative that is likely to strengthen Western economic and social cohesion, reinforce U.S. commitment to Europe, strengthen transatlantic energy ties, and contribute to greater attractiveness of the Western model. TTIP would also bolster the resilience of central and east European economies, stimulate U.S. investment and enable such countries to more easily resist Russian encroachment. These changes are likely to resonate across Wider Europe, especially Ukraine, Moldova, Georgia and even Belarus.

This is anathema to the current leadership in the Kremlin. TTIP presents a huge challenge to the Kremlin's efforts to divide Europeans from Americans. It offers something that the Kremlin cannot match: a transparent, mutually beneficial agreement that creates a rules-based framework for international cooperation. A reinvigorated transatlantic marketplace among highly-connected, highly-competitive democracies, whose people enjoy greater economic growth and rising standards of living, would challenge the Kremlin's version of "managed democracy;" render Russia's own one-dimensional natural-resource-based economic model increasingly unattractive; and consign its rival economic project, the Eurasian Economic Union, to irrelevance. Greater U.S.-EU energy cooperation would blunt Russia's monopolistic approach to European energy markets. And if such benefits extended to non-EU neighbors, particularly Ukraine, Russians themselves are likely to ask why their own country can't be better run.

For all these reasons, the Kremlin is conducting "active measures" in Eastern Europe, and in the EU itself, including tactics of pressure and intimidation, to derail the TTIP. The West should push back while indicating a readiness to engage with Russia economically on the basis of the very rules and procedures being advanced through the TTIP -- if Russia adheres to obligations it has made in the WTO and, in particular, with regard to the inviolability of borders and principles enshrined in the Helsinki Final Act. The West is not excluding Russia; Russia is excluding itself.

TTIP and the International Rules-Based Order - Standard-Makers or Standard-Takers?

Third, TTIP is a potentially important instrument to bolder the international rules-based order. Since World War II the United States and the evolving European Union, each in its own way, has been a steward of the international rules-based order. Yet as new powers rise, older powers rise again, and the West faces challenges at home, the prospect now looms that Europeans and Americans could become standard-takers rather than standard-makers.

Europeans and Americans share an interest in extending prosperity through multilateral trade liberalization. The December 2013 Bali agreement on trade facilitation is a sign that piecemeal progress can be made. But the overall Doha Round has been underway for almost a decade and has registered only marginal progress, with no final agreement in sight, and the WTO system is under challenge, especially from emerging growth markets that have benefited substantially from the system.

Given this situation, EU and U.S. officials are using TTIP to unblock the WTO Doha negotiations and jumpstart multilateral negotiations. There is precedence for this. When the

Uruguay Round stalled in the early 1990s, the United States, Canada and Mexico negotiated the North American Free Trade Agreement in just 14 months in 1992; it came into force in 1994. This plurilateral effort had a catalytic effect on the multilateral system; the Uruguay Round re-started and concluded successfully. The Information Technology Agreement negotiated by the United States and the EU also eventually became the basic multilateral agreement in this area. With the Doha Round stalled, we may again be at a point where plurilateral initiatives can ultimately reenergize the multilateral system.

Even a successful Doha Round agreement, however, would not address a host of issues that were not part of its mandate and yet are critical to the United States, the European Union, and the global economy. In this regard TTIP can be a pioneering effort to extend the multilateral system to new areas and new members. Each of TTIP's three pillars has the potential either to strengthen and expand multilateral rules (WTO-plus), or to generate standards and norms in new areas beyond the current system (WTO-extra).

The standards being negotiated as part of TTIP are intended to be more rigorous than comparable rules found in the WTO. Agreement on such issues as intellectual property, services, discriminatory industrial policies or state-owned enterprises could strengthen the normative underpinnings of the multilateral system by creating benchmarks for possible future multilateral liberalization under the WTO. U.S.-EU agreement on such principles, and agreement to act together to advance such norms globally, could not only take the international trading system further but establish broader political principles regarding the rule of law, human rights, labor, environmental and consumer standards.

As both President Obama and Congressional leaders in Congress have stated, if we don't write the rules of the global economy, somebody else will.

In short, TTIP promises significant advantages to U.S. national security and foreign policy. Yet TTIP could be even more significant if the United States and the EU would address three gaps in their current approach.

Three Missing Pieces

Energy

TTIP has become important in the context of changing transatlantic energy realities. More effective energy cooperation originally was not a major impetus for the talks, but should now be incorporated to facilitate U.S. energy exports to Europe as part of a more strategic transatlantic approach to energy cooperation.

Recent events in Ukraine and Russia have made clear that creating a transatlantic energy market is about more than economic efficiency. Energy cooperation has become an indispensable pillar of the Western community. Today the EU produces only a small portion of its energy needs, importing about 80% of its oil and about 60% of its gas. More than a third of this oil and 30% of the gas is of Russian origin. Some EU member states are 100% dependent on Russia for their gas needs.

Over the past few years America's oil and gas boom has rendered the United States over 80% self-sufficient in energy production and use. It will soon become an exporter of natural gas and surpass both Russia and Saudi Arabia to become the world's largest producer of oil and liquid natural gas.

A successful TTIP would enable the United States to export gas more easily to Europe, since U.S. law proscribes such exports/requires onerous licensing procedures except to countries with which the United States has a free trade agreement. In essence, members of the TTIP and the Trans-Pacific Partnership alike should be eligible for waivers to Department of Energy licensing requirements. In addition, TTIP could enable the United States and the EU to align standards in areas such as e-mobility and energy efficiency, reduce tariff and non-tariff barriers to clean energy goods and services, and create mechanisms for mutual recognition of regulatory processes regarding energy innovation. It also offers a mechanism for the United States and the EU to agree on basic normative principles that could have important global repercussions. One example is mandatory access for third parties to pipelines in the hands of a monopoly. Both U.S. and EU law provide for this, but if extended more broadly as an international norm it would have significant impact on countries such as Ukraine or those in Central Asia.

Some critics are skeptical that substantial U.S. energy could flow to Europe anytime soon, given the fact that it will take years to build appropriate new infrastructure to send and receive American gas. They also note that LNG from the United States will never flow to Europe in large enough quantities to replace the 160 billion cubic meters the EU imports from Russia.

Such criticisms miss the point that even small amounts of LNG can be important bargaining tools for countries otherwise dependent on Russia as a monopoly supplier; just the prospect of American gas flows to Europe has forced Russia to break the link between oil and gas prices and to negotiate better terms with a number of European customers, including in Germany, Poland and Lithuania. And while it will take time to build new infrastructure, likely investors are deciding today on such multi-year projects. A strong U.S.-EU political signal of intent to build a more strategic energy partnership, including through TTIP, can influence such investment decisions, even as it sends a strong message of transatlantic solidarity in the face of Russian troublemaking.

The Issue of Openness

A second issue also requires greater definition and clarity. Despite TTIP's inherent potential to leverage U.S-EU efforts to engage rising powers on the terms of their integration into the international rules-based order, governments have not stated whether and how the eventual TTIP agreement, once concluded, might be open to others willing and able to commit to similar goals and ground rules. USTR Mike Froman has characterized TTIP as an "open platform," but the two parties have made no official statement to this effect. This stands in contrast to the TPP, where the United States and its negotiating partners have stated explicitly that the TPP is open to other APEC members (including China and Russia) and in principle much of the Asia-Pacific region.

Framing the TTIP as an element of 'open architecture' accessible to others could give the West tremendous leverage in terms of ensuring ever broader commitment to the high standards and basic principles governing modern open economies, much as NATO and EU enlargement gave the West significant leverage over transitional democracies in central and eastern Europe. Once reason why many Turks are interested in TTIP, for instance, is that it represents a "transatlantic form of governance" rooted in the rule of law, as opposed to authoritarian or dirigiste models, and thus is important as a means to influence Turkey's own modernization.

The fact that the United States and the European Union have not yet stated that TTIP is part of an open architecture of trade, however, contributes to concern among other countries that TTIP is a "West against the rest" initiative, and thus more about trade diversion that trade creation. It invites counterbalancing coalitions and undermines TTIP's own rationale as a values-driven lever to open global markets.

As a first step, President Obama and EU leaders should issue a Leaders Statement that TTIP is part of an open architecture of trade. Such a Statement does not yet need to outline modalities. The Leaders Statement could also announce that the two parties are initiating consultative/information mechanisms for third parties potentially affected by a final agreement, recognizing that some of this is already underway.

Once such a Statement is made, further internal work should be done to make it operational. The underlying premise is that the TTIP package would be opened only after negotiated. On this basis, various options may be worth exploring. One is straightforward accession; countries that are willing and able to meet the same high standards as negotiated could accede. There may be an option to open individual elements to others, for instance market access or signing on to basic investment principles. This option would recognize that there are likely to be limits as to how open TTIP can be. For instance, it will be difficult simply to open some regulatory arrangements that might emerge from TTIP, or to open the "living agreement" aspect of a TTIP process, because such elements are likely to be based on trust and confidence generated among U.S. and EU regulators, legislators and certifiers. But countries may be able to join or attach themselves to some provisions. For instance, when the United States and EU finalized their Open Skies agreement on transatlantic air transport in 2007, legal texts were created enabling a range of additional countries, not only in Europe but in other parts of the world, to also implement provisions of the agreement through separate accords.

Special arrangements might be needed for countries like Turkey, which has a Customs Union with the EU but nothing similar with the United States; EFTA countries Switzerland, Norway,

Iceland and Liechtenstein, with related arrangements with the EU; and NAFTA members Mexico and Canada. The issue of "open architecture" also has great resonance for Ukraine, Moldova and Georgia, with which the EU has signed Deep and Comprehensive Free Trade Agreements, and whose stability and prosperity is linked to U.S. interest in a Europe whole and free.

Another variant might be for the United States and the EU to negotiate new or additional WTO-compatible agreements. There is some precedent for this option as well. For instance, since Chile could not accede to NAFTA, the United States negotiated a separate bilateral arrangement.

Whatever modalities are chosen, after the agreement is concluded the two parties should be proactive about making "open architecture" real.

Addressing Concerns of Poorer Countries

A related consideration has to do with how the United States and the EU approach poorer countries. Much depends on the way the two handle the multiple trade agreements that each has with third countries and regions. They would do well to send an early signal that the TTIP is about common efforts to open markets by harmonizing their current hodgepodge of trade preference mechanisms for low-income African countries.

Sub-Saharan Africa, the poorest region in the world, accounts for a minuscule 2 percent of world trade. This marginalization of the region is holding back its development at a time when its economic governance is rapidly improving. Sub-Saharan Africa needs generous access to developed consumer markets to spur investment in labor-intensive export sectors that can spark growth and contribute to its successful economic transformation.

Both the United States and the European Union give trade preferences for (some) products from (some) countries in sub-Saharan Africa. The EU provides duty-free and quota-free access to its markets for all products — but only to the 27 least-developed countries in the region. It also offers less generous access to former colonies through preferential deals. The U.S. scheme benefits 40 of the 48 countries in the region, but excludes key agricultural products (such as cotton) that African countries can produce competitively. These schemes may look good on paper, but they are actually underutilized because of their administrative complexity and outdated rules. Local content requirements are too high, and the rules of origin required for product eligibility were created decades before the development of today's value chains, which involve many countries specializing in fragmented tasks. Moreover, the United States and the EU use different methods to define origin, forcing exporters to cope with a myriad of rules.

It will be difficult to justify or implement a North Atlantic deal in which the participants have differing rules for developing countries. What foreign policy interest is served, for example, if the EU and the United States provide different access to Kenya's products? In addition, once a

Transatlantic Marketplace is in place it will make no sense to have differing access arrangements for companies from third countries. The United States and the European Union could gain considerable political advantage while following through on the logical consequence of their own negotiations by harmonizing their trade preference schemes for sub-Saharan Africa, either as part of or as a complement to their partnership pact.

As the Congress considers new legislation regarding the African Growth and Opportunities Act, it would do well to consider this issue.

In other writings, my colleague Eveline Herfkens and I, together with K.Y. Amaoko, President of the African Center for Economic Transformation suggest that a new transatlantic deal for the poorest African countries would do well by covering all products, since excluding just a few could encompass most products that these countries can produce competitively. Rules of origin need to be relevant, simple and flexible for beneficiaries to be able to use the schemes and benefit from the growth of value chains. Such value chains have virtually bypassed the region so far, but they hold considerable potential for less-developed African countries. It is much easier for these countries to develop capabilities in a narrow range of tasks than in integrated production of entire products or processes.

Updating these rules to the realities of 21st century production networks is long overdue. WTO negotiations on clarifying rules of origin are likely to take decades; the United States and the EU could do something together now. As an interim solution the European Union and the United States could recognize each other's origin regime. If an import is eligible for preferential treatment in America, it should be also in Europe, and vice versa. By acting now, the United States and the European Union would also demonstrate that TTIP is about opening markets rather than diverting trade.

Conclusion

TTIP is ambitious. It will be tough to conclude. But the potential payoff is high, and the geostrategic impact of such an agreement could be as profound as the direct economic benefits. If legislators and executives on both sides of the Atlantic grasp the moment, they may well become best known for having re-founded the Atlantic Partnership. If they do not, then issues of failing trust and confidence, so visible today, will continue to eat away at America's premier alliance like termites in the woodwork.

Mr. POE. Thank all of our witnesses. I will yield 5 minutes to myself for some questions and then we will move through the panel as well.

Big scheme of things, I believe in free trade and trade with countries throughout the world for all the reasons we have talked about. The problem is always, as my friends have said, the devil is in the details. There may be something in an agreement that we don't like for a lot of reasons, politically, economically, human rights, whatever. We have got TPA that I think, Ambassador, you said has been approved 18 times in the last 30, 40, 60, 80 years.

Ambassador HILLS. Seventy years.

Mr. POE. Seventy years. Thank you, Ambassador. And then we have TTIP and TPP. We start with the Trade Promotion Authority. Congress has to approve that and there is some cynicism in Congress because we can't get much information from the administration. We have asked the administration eight times to testify before our Committee on Foreign Affairs. I had spoken with Mr. Froman. Michael Froman, in 2013, was the first time he promised me he would give me a private briefing. Well, we haven't had it yet. So there is some skepticism or suspicion, if you will, about what has taken place because Congress then has the problem of well, do we give the administration the TPA, the Trade Promotion Authority, even though we are not really getting much information out of the administration on what the end game is with these two trade agreements?

Ambassador, can you help us out a little bit about what is going on with the administration and whether we should press that issue a little more or is that just the way it is?

Ambassador HILLS. I have to say when I served, I spent a good time with my friends on the Hill, both in this body and in the Senate. I found having executive sessions with those who were interested, and often it is hard to get Congress to be interested, an executive session is useful. And I say that because when you are negotiating, whether you are negotiating to buy your house or your car, you want to keep your negotiations not public. You don't want them on the front page of the newspaper so the persons you are negotiating with know what your strategy is. But Congress and the Executive Branch must have a collaborative arrangement. I can tell you it works.

I could not have done the negotiations that we did without my friends on the Hill. They understood that it was necessary not to publicize so widely what we were trying to get from multiple governments. Because what you want to get from Government A may offend Government B, and so any negotiation requires some degree of discretion.

I would encourage you to have executive sessions and I am certainly happy to encourage Mr. Froman to meet more often with you. I am shocked that you say you have not seen him since 2013.

Mr. POE. For a briefing, that is correct. I appreciate that insight and going on, moving on to the specifics of the two agreements, let me just talk about Europe.

Dr. Hamilton, anybody else can weigh in on this as well. When I visited Ukraine, the President told me that he sure would like to see some natural gas coming from the United States. In 2009, I think, the Russians turned the gas off for 2 weeks in the winter. It was cold because I happened to be there for part of that time. I understand the economic hostage that the Europeans feel. You can hear it in what they say because they are very careful about saying things to me, it seems like, to not offend the Russians because they are getting their energy from them.

So just theory, not the details of an agreement with transatlantic partnership, how would that help economically Europe, but also help economically the United States if we dealt with energy, for example.

Mr. HAMILTON. Thank you, Mr. Chairman. Well, you are absolutely right. Energy is a really important part of this relationship. The quick answer would be that a TTIP would enable us to go around some of those onerous requirements you mentioned, the Department of Energy and so on because if we have a free trade agreement with partners, much of that opens up. But it doesn't quite do the job.

My critique of the current TTIP is that there is a discussion about a proposed energy chapter, but both sides have not quite embraced it. And it is not only about free flow of energy in the trade sense because many on the U.S. side would say well, if we get the trade deal it frees up all of those problems, so what is the issue? Why do we have to have a chapter? I think it goes more to this point about standards and norms.

If we could agree across the Atlantic on some basic principles governing energy trade to strengthen the rules-based order, that would become core, global benchmarks. And Ukraine is a good example. We have currently, across the Atlantic, for instance, noncontroversial, a basic principle that when a monopoly owns a pipeline, third parties have mandatory access to that pipeline. That we agree. In the United States, we agree. In the EU, it is not a global principle. And you can imagine if we could enshrine that as a principle what it would mean for a country like Ukraine because it would start to raise the bar in terms of how we engage. So setting the bar higher, because of how we work with Europeans is really an important part of TTIP. It goes beyond opening up just the transatlantic market, but we could do that at the same. That would provide huge benefits for U.S. energy producers.

You see the other argument was about Asian prices being far higher than in Europe, but that has now changed. And the political signal to those who have to invest in infrastructure over a 5-, 10-year period happens today. They don't invest for 5, 10 years if they don't get the political signal now. And that is why the third element of why that is so important.

Mr. POE. Thank you, Dr. Hamilton. My time has expired. I will yield to the ranking member from Massachusetts, Mr. Keating.

Mr. KEATING. Thank you, Mr. Chairman. TPP is supposed to help address the U.S. trade issues with China and China has a long-term history of currency manipulation. During the time that TPP has been under negotiations at least 60 senators and 230 members of the House have called for binding currency disciplines to be included in the TPP. As far as I am aware, U.S. negotiators have not even introduced language related to currency, much less secure its approval from other TPP parties.

If the TPP lacks enforceable currency rules, it seems China and other manipulators would be free to conduct business as usual. How then will TPP be an example of the U.S. writing the rules? And is the freedom to game the system by manipulating currency really a rule we want to promote? I will let any of the panelists address that.

Mr. GREEN. Thank you. Our goal with China over the long run should not be to increase government control of currency. Our goal should be gradually for China to move toward more of a market-based currency so that the value of the renminbi reflects what is fair and economically logical. So I would think in our negotiating strategy we should be taking measures that encourage that move toward market-oriented factors, and in a broad sense TPP and TTIP will do that and will reinforce those within the People's Bank of China or within the Chinese system who also think that their current policies are a trap for them. They can't manipulate monetary policy effectively with the current currency strategy that they have. It is a longer-term game with China that I think should be shaped by market-base rules.

And the other thing about currency manipulation, I would say, is the G7, the G20, the IMF have acknowledged that a lot of us, including the United States and Japan, have engaged in monetary using to get out of the financial crisis, the economic crisis we were all in and in Japan's case to get out of deflation. And I think that is sort of self-policing process that is quite effective in these international financial meetings and organizations. There is legislation, of course, for the Treasury Department to report on currency manipulation and that would be an area to focus, I think, if there were concerns going forward.

Mr. KEATING. What would be the harm in having that kind of language inserted? Why is that not addressed? Why do you suppose that that is not in the agreement?

Ambassador HILLS. In my own view, the trade agreement should try to open the market and create opportunity. We have institutions like the IMF and the G20 that can focus on currency. We have been using our currency to try to stimulate our economy. We would react poorly in my humble opinion, if other countries or even an institution were to tell us that we should back off. So I think that our trade agreements, both TPP and TTIP, should seek to open opportunities.

You mentioned jobs in your opening remarks. And I was struck by the fact that even with the 28 nations that make up Europe, we are losing competitiveness because of regulatory turmoil. And by having harmonization, we will help small- and medium-sized businesses that are responsible for 90 percent of the new jobs. There are many small businesses in the United States that do not export to countries that speak their language, that want their product, because they cannot handle the paperwork.

Mr. GREEN. I would, of course, agree and the only thing I would add is that in these agreements, these kinds of mechanisms are always reciprocal. So we may have a mature and fair and market-oriented sense of whether there is currency manipulation, but our partners in these agreements will also have the opportunity to set up triggers. And we will lose control of that if we are not careful.

So we have a system with the IMF, the G20, the G7 that is effective that works for us. There is the legislation on treasury reporting, but we want to be careful about accidentally arming our trading partners with things that would be used against us with far more devastating effect than we might consider using them ourselves.

Mr. KEATING. Great. Thank you. I yield back. My time is up.

Mr. POE. I thank the ranking member. The chair will recognize the gentleman from California, Mr. Issa, for his questions.

Mr. ISSA. Thank you. And it is really a pleasure to have you here.

Ambassador, I will start with you. During the NAFTA era, first Canada, then Mexico, I think we discovered something which is even when people say they are for free and fair trade, everyone has something that is missing that needs to be included. When we did Canada, the labor unions didn't have a problem because the AFL–CIO moves across those borders transparently. Even though there are very strong unions in Mexico, lo and behold, if U.S. unions were not welcome, then they objected.

Moving forward though, we have in the case of Europe, for example, partners who join NATO and pay a very small share. They want common defense and in some cases to even join us in defense of our world liberties, but they do so at about half as much contribution. These have never been part of trade agreements. In other words, we talk about harmonization—and I am concerned—but whose harmonization? If it is not explicit within the bill at the time that Congress approves it, then are we harmonizing the European Union changing laws? That is what I want to get to.

The European Union is and I will be in Brussels in a couple of days, and someone will note that I have said this, but the European Union is an unfair trading partner because they do create nontariff trade barriers all the time and they do it systematically.

Do you believe that the administration can effectively create at least an arbitration capability so when they put up nontariff trade barriers, time and time again, and we will just use the fact that you can't sell an oil unless you can certify that the container that carried the oil, vegetable oil, never had a GMO in it. Okay. Now the absurdity of—by the way, it wouldn't matter if it wasn't consumed or not, whether it was being frying oil or anything. They wanted none of it.

Those sort of decisions are currently available to the Europeans. They use them regularly. Today, they are trying to break up Google. They have a number of those. So I guess my question is it used to be trade was all about trade. Then it became trade plus union considerations under the guise of human rights. Then it became environmental in addition to that. Should we also look at the regulatory burdens that may be placed on our companies when they do try to export in a low tariff environment and find these nontariff trade barriers being erected? Is that something the administration should be putting into trade agreements, at least the process?

Ambassador HILLS. Actually, the focus of the TTIP is to get regulatory harmony and the greatest amount of economic benefit will come not from tariff reduction, although you will get some of that.

Because our average tariffs are about 3 percent, we had several dozen that are very high.

Mr. ISSA. Have you ever tried to import a leather jacket? You are going to find out that there is like 12 different tariffs we still have in place.

Ambassador HILLS. But the regulatory problem, you know, you want to buy a car and you want to sell a car, we have different rules for the lights, the steering wheel, the windows going up and down.

Mr. ISSA. Let me get you on that, because that is perfect. You were there during the NAFTA negotiations. Mexico agreed to allow our automobiles in under specific requirements including an unlimited amount of early automobiles. Mexico has systemically tried to prevent those after the fact and today they are preventing the export of older U.S. cars which—some of which have been salvaged and so on. There is no question. But they are preventing it in spite of an agreement in NAFTA and their guise is that these are polluting. So even in the case of our agreement with Mexico, Mexico simply has disregarded elements of the trade agreement and we have no enforcement mechanism for it.

And I bring this up because I support free trade, but I also watched China sign on to the WTO and then ignore it; Russia get into the WTO and then ignore it. These countries are right now exporting, if you will, more great American movies than we do. The problem is they were originally ours.

Ambassador HILLS. Well, let me focus on your point about Mexico. Our trade with Mexico has gone up five fold. Our small- and medium-size businesses——

Mr. ISSA. And I am totally there for that. I came and I argued on behalf of the chamber for it. But it is not a question of successes. The question is when they selectively, any trade partner, uses a tactic including one explicitly prohibited, do we demand that the administration put from past experience arbitration or other capability to stop it? Like I say, it doesn't matter how much you trade with Mexico, if you tried to export a few hundred thousand cars that are surplus in the U.S., older cars, you will find out Mexico won't take them even though they signed an agreement saying they clearly would.

Ambassador HILLS. What Mexico has agreed to is to give national treatment. And they do not have a surplus of old cars. The same pollution standards——

Mr. ISSA. Ma'am, ma'am. Have you been to Mexico lately? There are so many old Volkswagens driving around there, they simply don't want our new old Volkswagens.

Ambassador HILLS. What I was about to say is that the pollution standards for those coming into Mexico and those that are there are the same. They are given national treatment. If someone is exporting and feels they are not getting national treatment and they are being discriminated against, yes, there must be a mechanism for resolving that dispute. That has not been a primary problem with Mexico. Our trade has increased. Our investment has increased. In fact, most manufacturers and particularly, small and medium size manufacturers, will say that they not only sell things to one another back and forth across our northern and southern borders, they make things together.

Mr. ISSA. I was only asking you, should in a trade agreement there be a mechanism if a company claims that to be true? The fact is, it is true and we do have the companies that have found these changes that unfairly, essentially after the fact, decide they are no longer going to take American cars.

Ambassador HILLS. Is a mechanism?

Mr. ISSA. Okay, so you do believe it should be there and it should be enforceable?

Ambassador HILLS. There is a mechanism in all agreements. NAFTA has one. The WTO has one.

Mr. POE. The gentleman's time has expired.

Mr. ISSA. Thank you, Mr. Chairman.

Mr. POE. The chair recognizes the gentleman from California, Mr. Sherman, for his questions.

Mr. SHERMAN. Thank you. All the advocates of these agreements talk about exports, but they don't subtract out imports, so then they argue that if we export $1 billion and import $2 billion that is great because we have got $3 billion in trade. The fact is if exports create jobs, imports take them away. That is why the change in our trade policy that began in the late 1980s has accompanied the total destruction of the American middle class.

We focus just on the jobs we lose. But that is not the sole focus. It is keeping wages down. First, an employer says—and the Ambassador was talking about how employers love this because they can say we are going to cut wages or we are going to move the jobs. We will open up a new plant or the nicer ones say, we have got to keep wages low because we face free access to the U.S. market from 50-cent-an-hour Vietnam labor. So we have got to keep wages low.

Then some factories shut down. That creates more workers. Supply and demand, that keeps wages down. And then states see that wages are down, the supply of workers is up, we had an economic crisis, so they become right to work states and then no unions, no raises. And so the decimation of the middle class has been accomplished before we even lose many jobs. But of course, we have lost millions and millions. So the American people aren't going to allow us to do this unless we fool them and tell them it is about national security because they know it hurts our country.

Now we are told that this is an anti-China system that we are creating. Well, wait a minute, the same advocates are the ones who advocated the worst trade deal we ever had permanent, most favored nation status with China. So we enter into that agreement in the late 1990s. We give away millions of jobs to China which strengthens them to the point where in order to repair the geopolitical problem we have to give millions of jobs to China's neighbors. So first you give the jobs to China, strengthen them, and then give the jobs to China's neighbors to strengthen them. Everybody is strong except America and our families.

Then we are told that we will deprive ourselves of the great honor of defending Japanese and Korean islets. They are really uninhabited rocks at great expense to the United States. For the benefit of countries in the case of Japan, it has spent less than 1 percent of their own money on their national defense. So we will lose the chance to spend hundreds of billions of dollars protecting islets which, if they have any oil, and they don't, it is not our oil. But everything going on at the Air Force and Navy is how can we spend hundreds of billions of dollars in our research and procurement to prepare ourselves to protect these islets and oh, by the way, let us give away millions of jobs so that we will have the opportunity and be invited to provide this defense of rocks for free.

No wonder all of Wall Street is for this deal and all of America is against it. Although given the amount of money that has been spent to propagandize to the American people, I guess it is not surprising as many as one third could be fooled into supporting this agreement.

My question is we are told that we have got to include Vietnam in this agreement. We know we might have to include Vietnam, because that is the 50 cent an hour labor that will make sure we can really drive wages down in the United States, but that is not the given reason. We are told we have to include Vietnam because we will get free access to their markets, but of course, Vietnam has no freedom and they have no markets.

Dr. Green, is there any evidence that by signing this agreement, the Vietnamese Government and its Communist Party will not be in control of all major exports, $1-billion contracts, $100-million contracts of American goods entering Vietnam? Do they lose control so that some business person can contradict party policy safely and import American goods?

Mr. GREEN. So this is an important question and I think it is good that the ranking member and that you and others are focused on it because we have an important stake not only in our economic relationship with Vietnam, but with the improvement of governance, human rights, and democracy in these countries. I have been disturbed that the U.S. Government spending on governance and human rights and democracy has dropped almost in half in the past 8 or 9 years. I just mention that because trade is not the answer for all these problems. There are other tools we need to bring to this, but I think it is an important question.

I worked for 5 years in the NSC for President Bush on Asia. Went to Vietnam to press these issues. Vietnam reformed about halfway, the so-called Doi Moi reforms. So about half of the Vietnamese economy is government dominated and about half is moving toward a much more free market direction. We definitely have an interest in terms of economics, strategic relations and human rights and democracy in spreading that nongovernmental sector.

Mr. SHERMAN. Do you think that a business person in Vietnam, when they get a call from the Communist Party saying don't buy the American goods, oh yes, we have published our reduction in tariffs. Oh, yes, we have signed written agreements, but we are telling you on the phone don't buy the goods, that that businessman is going to call a press conference, denounce the Communist Party and announce how he is being pressured? Can you imagine that happening in Vietnam? Or is what is much more likely the businessman will say, "Yes, sir. I will buy the German goods if you think that is better. I will buy the Chinese goods if you think that is better. I will do whatever the party wants."

Can you point to one case where someone in control of a $100-million enterprise in Vietnam has stood up and denounced party interference in their import and export decisions? And it is never going to happen, is it, because they are going to be killed.

Mr. GREEN. But is there a case where an American CEO has stood up and condemned policy in the United States that doesn't directly affect their business? I would say this though——

Mr. SHERMAN. Well, I am talking about something that would affect their business and yes, there are plenty of business people that condemn our foreign policy every day from both angles. I hear from them every day. I know my time has expired, but the idea that you are going to have labor rights in Vietnam, that you are going to have free markets in Vietnam, that no one is going to be disappeared in Vietnam, is something you can believe only if you are so dedicated to this agreement that your eyes are closed. I yield back.

Mr. GREEN. So I spent time on the ground in Hanoi.

Mr. POE. Briefly comment or answer that.

Mr. GREEN. Thank you, Mr. Chairman. I spent time on the ground in Vietnam, working to expand the number of house churches, to end the prosecution of Catholic bishops and parochial schools when in government and we had success. Why? In part because at the time we were negotiating normal trade relations. We had considerable leverage (a), and (b) because the Chinese ultimately did not want to fall into China's orbit.

So we have leverage and we have an opportunity now to influence this and no, Vietnamese business leaders are not standing up and condemning the Communist Party, but many, many more Vietnamese than Chinese are on the internet and in other ways protesting their government as they have more opportunities and more choices.

Mr. SHERMAN. Dr. Green, every single group in America dedicated to human rights in Vietnam says vote no on TTP. I yield back.

Mr. POE. I thank the gentleman from California. He yielded back twice, so I will take it the second time. I thank all of you for being here. You can see that this is an important issue for all the members up here. Our opinions vary tremendously. We will see how it ends up down the road, but thank you for your time and thank you for your testimony. The subcommittee is adjourned.

[Whereupon, at 3:15 p.m., the subcommittee was adjourned.]

APPENDIX

Material Submitted for the Record

SUBCOMMITTEE HEARING NOTICE
COMMITTEE ON FOREIGN AFFAIRS
U.S. HOUSE OF REPRESENTATIVES
WASHINGTON, DC 20515-6128

Subcommittee on Terrorism, Nonproliferation, and Trade
Ted Poe (R-TX), Chairman

TO: MEMBERS OF THE COMMITTEE ON FOREIGN AFFAIRS

You are respectfully requested to attend an OPEN hearing of the Committee on Foreign Affairs, to be held by the Subcommittee on Terrorism, Nonproliferation, and Trade in Room 2172 of the Rayburn House Office Building (and available live on the Committee website at http://www.ForeignAffairs.house.gov):

DATE: Tuesday, March 17, 2015

TIME: 2:00 p.m.

SUBJECT: National Security Benefits of Trade Agreements with Asia and Europe

WITNESSES: The Honorable Carla A. Hills
                   Co-Chairman
                   Council on Foreign Relations
                   (Former U.S. Trade Representative)

                   Michael J. Green, Ph.D.
                   Senior Vice President for Asia and Japan Chair
                   Center for Strategic and International Studies

                   Daniel S. Hamilton, Ph.D.
                   Director
                   Center for Transatlantic Relations
                   The Paul H. Nitze School of Advanced International Studies
                   Johns Hopkins University

By Direction of the Chairman

The Committee on Foreign Affairs seeks to make its facilities accessible to persons with disabilities. If you are in need of special accommodations, please call 202/225-5021 at least four business days in advance of the event, whenever practicable. Questions with regard to special accommodations in general (including availability of Committee materials in alternative formats and assistive listening devices) may be directed to the Committee.

COMMITTEE ON FOREIGN AFFAIRS

MINUTES OF SUBCOMMITTEE ON _____*Terrorism Nonproliferation and Trade*_____ HEARING

Day___*Tuesday*___ Date___*March 17, 2015*___ Room_____*2172*_____

Starting Time ___*2:00 p.m.*___ Ending Time ___*3:15 p.m.*___

Recesses |___| (___to___) (___to___) (___to___) (___to___) (___to___) (___to___)

Presiding Member(s)

Chairman Ted Poe

Check all of the following that apply:

Open Session ☑   Electronically Recorded (taped) ☑
Executive (closed) Session ☐   Stenographic Record ☑
Televised ☑

TITLE OF HEARING:

"National Security Benefits of Trade Agreements with Asia and Europe"

SUBCOMMITTEE MEMBERS PRESENT:

Reps. Poe, Issa, Perry, Keating, Sherman, Kelly

NON-SUBCOMMITTEE MEMBERS PRESENT: *(Mark with an * if they are not members of full committee.)*

HEARING WITNESSES: Same as meeting notice attached? Yes ☑ **No** ☐
(If "no", please list below and include title, agency, department, or organization.)

STATEMENTS FOR THE RECORD: *(List any statements submitted for the record.)*

TIME SCHEDULED TO RECONVENE _____
or
TIME ADJOURNED ___*3:15 p.m.*___

_____
Subcommittee Staff Director